THE CODE ACADEMY

PRESENTS

Python Programming

An In-Depth Guide Into The Essentials
Of
Python Programming

Table of Contents

1. Chapter 1: Introduction

You have used a computer. You even own one or more, and it helps you accomplish all kinds of interesting and useful things. The many applications that computers run to help you solve daily life problems to make your life easier are designed and written by programmers to accept input and respond to commands in different ways—but you already know this.

The underlying operations that make computer applications and computer systems in general useful are determined by the design in which the programs are written. In this eBook, you will learn how to write computer programs so that a user can issue instructions to the computer and make it react a way that solves their problems. This eBook will teach you the basics on how to write computer programs using a programming language called Python.

What is Python?

Python is one of the numerous computer programming languages that are gaining popularity every day. It is a general high-level language that is easy to learn and even easier to use. Its style and philosophy emphasizes on code readability and simplicity. The syntax makes it easy for programmers to write computer instructions in fewer lines of code compared to the number it would take to write similar instructions in other languages such as Java, C++, or C#.

Python's core philosophy is summarized in the first seven principles that governed the development of the language as written in The Zen of Python: They read:

1. Beautiful is better than ugly.

2. Explicit is better than implicit.

3. Simple is better than complex.

4. Complex is better than complicated.

5. Flat is better than nested.

6.   Sparse is better than dense.

7.   Readability counts.

At the risk of exposing my biasness towards the language, I will make a bold claim that Python is fast and steadily becoming the most popular programming language amongst beginner programmers. You probably chose to study this language because you were influenced by a programmer already using it, or learning it. You are in luck because you get to study a simple-to-learn yet powerful programming language that is also economical with a high level information structure.

Studying Python is possibly the most effective approach you could have chosen to learn object-oriented programming. The code you will learn to create by studying the chapters in this eBook will help you create elegant and dynamic syntax that is already interpreted. Your code will be perfect and ready for scripting, and turning simple lines of text into speedy and useful applications that can run on a variety of platforms – both small and large scale. Whether you are completely new to computer programming or have some experience with another language, you will be pleasantly surprised how easy it is to create powerful programs with Python.

What should you expect of this book?

This book is written for a complete beginner to the world of programming or a seasoned programmer curious to learn a new language. It goes deep to show what makes Python such a dynamic programming language, starting from how to set it up on your computer, what the different data types it uses are, what basic functions you need to know, and what classes and objects are used in the course of creating programs. It also teaches the basics about operators and variables, and how to call functions among others.

Do not be intimidated by all these jargon—they are the most basic things you need to learn when you are introduced to any programming language. What makes this book special, however, is **HOW** you learn them, and not **WHAT** you learn. You could use Google only and still get as much information as you need to get started, but you would probably end up lost and confused because you need ordered and simplified introduction to master the art of coding in Python.

This book uses instruction technique to guide you through a sequence of 64 controlled exercises that will build your skills through practice. First you do, see **HOW** it works, then learn the **WHAT** and **WHY.** This is a great way to gradually but progressively establish your coding skills by practice and memorization, which enables you to apply what you learn in more difficult problems at the end of each section of the book.

By the end of this book, you will be equipped with the skills to learn even more complex programming topics in Python and other object oriented programming languages. As long as you invest your focus in every chapter of the book, dedicate some time in understanding and practicing what you learn, and apply the skills you acquire outside what you learn within the book, you will be a proficient Python programmer in no time.

What you need to get started

The requirements to use this book to learn programming using Python are pretty straightforward:

1. You must have a computer running a Windows, Mac OS, or Linux.

    To be able to write computer programs in Python, you need to have a compatible operating system with Python binaries installed. Some operating systems including Mac OS and Linux come with Python pre-installed, but you may need to download and install from python.org if your system has the older v. 2 installed or if you are a Windows user.

    There are two versions of Python currently in use: Python 2.x and Python 3.x or simply Python 2 and Python 3. There are subtle differences between these two versions that may nevertheless affect how your program runs, hence how you write your scripts. Ensure that you have Python 3 installed in your system before you proceed. Go to https://wiki.python.org/moin/BeginnersGuide/Download to learn more about this.

2. **You must know basic computer operations and how to read and write.**

Stupidly obvious as it may seem, you need to have basic computer skills that include typing and manipulating files and folders to become a programmer. If you have not used a computer before, this book is not for you. You cannot learn to create computer software if you have not used computer software before. Considering how far you have come, this book assumes that you can read, write, and follow simple instructions.

3. **You must pay attention to detail and be persistent**

What typically sets good computer programmers apart from bad programmers is how they can visually spot minute differences between two pieces of text. For instance, you must be able to tell the difference between a colon (:) and a semicolon (;) because it can be the difference between a functional and buggy code. Unless you learn to pay close attention to detail, you will miss key elements that make your program what you want it to be.

While studying to become a programmer, you will make many mistakes, just the way musicians make many mistakes when learning to play the guitar. But getting it wrong once should not mean the end of the road for you; you must persist and go over your code over and over to understand it or to find problems in them. Repetitive practice is what will make you good at writing computer programs.

Setting up Python environment

On your computer, open a terminal window and type the word "python" to find out if the local environment is already set up and which version is installed. If you do not have the latest version of Python installed, you can download the source code, binaries and documentation for Python 3.5 from python.org.

You will need to know whether you are running a 32-bit or a 64-bit operating system beforehand to download the right version of Python for your computer.

Should you encounter any difficulty while downloading or installing the program (package for unix-based systems), you can check out the simplified beginner's resources on this link:
https://wiki.python.org/moin/BeginnersGuide .

By default, Python creates an installation directory on the root of your computer hard drive with a name that corresponds to the version number of the Python development environment you downloaded. For instance, Python 3.6.2 release candidate 1 installs to C:\Python36-21\ on a Windows computer. You can change where Python installs by clicking on "Customize installation" button during setup.

Be sure to check the '*Add Python 3.5 to PATH*' option during the last step of setup.

When Python installs successfully to your computer, you will be able to write scripts in Python as instructed in this book and run them with no problem. We recommend that you extract the practice Exercise files bundled with the book to the '**Exercises**' directory within the Python installation folder to make it easy to execute them during the course of learning. The path to the Exercises directory will look something like this:

C:\Python36-21\Exercises\

This is also the location you should save your practice files for easier access from the terminal.

The Python shell

When you install Python, you will have the option to run python scripts saved as **.py** files right from your computer's terminal or you can use the simpler Python IDLE integrated development environment. When you install Python, a link to IDLE link will be placed on the desktop or your programs menu. We use the command-line interpreter for exercises in this book because it is more practical and helps you learn and master concepts faster with less distractions.

You can initialize the Python Shell via the IDLE link placed on the desktop, on the dock if you use a Mac, or on the Start menu if you are a windows user.

Use a text editor

You need a text editor to write your code on and save it as a **.py**. Word processors such as MS Word will not work because they introduce formatting characters in the text that will interfere with the code. There are many lightweight text editors you can download and install that come with advanced tools to check and even color your code to minimize the chances of making mistakes.

Some of the most popular text editors you should check out are Notepad++, Vim, Atom, Sublime Text, and Text Wrangler for Mac users.

Executing Python scripts

Python scripts have an extension of **.py**. When saving your code, be sure to specify this in the filename. It is preferable that you save your exercise scripts with a simple but descriptive name with no spaces. The exercise files accompanying this book are named **Exercise1.py, Exercise2.py** and so on.

Proper naming of your script files eliminates chances of errors and confusion when calling them from the terminal.

To run the saved **.py** scripts, you will need to know a few things about navigating the terminal (the command line interface). The instructions are much alike for navigating the terminal is similar for most operating systems. You should know how to change directories (you must always be on the working directory in which the python scripts are saved to call them), and you should know how to call and quit the Python interpreter.

To call the Python interpreter, simply type **Python**.

If typing Python calls the interpreter for the older version 2 Python interpreter, you may want to try **Python3**, especially if you are a Linux or Mac user.

For instance, to run a script saved as HelloWorld.py on a windows terminal, you will enter this on your terminal then press enter:

```
C:\Python36-21\Exercises\Python HelloWorld.py
```

Now that we have that out of the way, let us begin.

Chapter 2. Python Basic Syntax Rules, Variables and Values

Hello World Program

In keeping with the age-old tradition of introducing newbies to the world of programming with a simple Hello World, your first program will be a simple program that displays the "Hello World".

First off, start your command line terminal and initiate the Python interpreter by typing "python" and pressing enter. You should see a prompt with three arrows meaning that the Python interpreter has been invoked.

Enter the following text and press enter (return):

```
>>> print ("Hello World!")
```

This is a way to invoke the interpreter without having to pass a script file. However, this approach does not save your program because the code is interpreted and executed from the temporary memory.

To create a program we can save, we will have to save the line of code we typed in a **.py** script file using a text editor.

Exercise1: Hello World!

Start your text editor and type the code as it appears, replacing the (enter your name here) with your name. Choose a name to save your script as, such as **HelloWorld.py**. The line of code on your editor should look like this:

```
print ("Hello World!") #This will display Hello World! text on the screen
print ('Hello World again!')
print ("My name is (enter your name here)")
```

If you set the Python PATH variable correctly during setup, you should be able to run the saved **.py** script from the terminal by typing this command:

```
$ python HelloWorld.py
```

If you typed the code exactly as it appears, and you are running Python from the directory in which the python script is saved, you should see the following result on your terminal when you execute the **HelloWorld.py** script:

```
print ("Hello World!") #This will display Hello World! text on the screen
print ('Hello World again!')
print ("My name is (enter your name here)")
```

Congratulations! You just wrote your first program in Python! By your own effort, you have earned the right to be referred to as a programmer.

Basic Syntax Rules in Python

Before we can delve further into learning to write code in Python, there are a few universal Python syntax rules you must grasp first. In this section, we will cover the most basic rules you need to get started with your very first real Python program. We will learn more rules and best practices later on in the book.

Python Identifiers

An identifier is a name used to identify an object such as a variable, module, class, or function. In the Python language, an identifier must begin with an alphabetic letter in uppercase (A to Z), lower case (a to z) or an underscore (_) followed more letters, underscores, or numeric digits. Python does not allow the use of punctuation characters such as %, /, $, or @ within the identifier name.

It is also important to note that Python is a case sensitive language. This means that an identifier **age** is not the same as **Age**.

Reserved Words

There are a number of words written in lowercase letters that are reserved and cannot be used as constants, variables, or variable identifies. Here is a table of these words:

And	assert	break	class	continue
Def	del	elif	else	except
exec	finally	for	from	global
If	import	in	is	lambda
Not	or	pass	print	raise
return	try	while	with	yield

Table 1: Reserved words in Python.

Lines and Indentation

Unlike most other object-oriented programming languages, Python does not make use of curly braces to group lines of code into blocks to define functions, classes and flow control structures. Instead, line indentations are used to denote blocks of code. The rule of indentation is rigidly enforced.

The number of spaces in the indentation may vary, but all statements within one block must have matching indentation spaces, typically four spaces or one tab per indent level.

Multi-Line Statements

Typically, statements in Python end with a new line. However, the line continuation character (\) can be used to denote that the line does not end and instead continues in the next. Consider this example:

```
Total_cost = item1_price + \
        item2_price + \
        item3_price
```

Multi-line statements contained within brackets (), square brackets [], or curly braces {} do not need the line continuation character.

```
workdays = ["Monday", "Tuesday", "Wednesday",
        "Thursday", " Friday", "Saturday"]
```

String Quotation Characters

Single ('), double ("), and triple ("' or """) quotation marks are used to denote string literals in Python. A quotation must start and end with the same type of quote mark. Triple quotation marks denote strings that may span multiple lines. In Exercise2, you can see how:

Exercise2: String quotation

```
name = 'John'
occupation = "Python programmer"
comment = """John is a Python programmer. He is
currently based in London."""

print (name)
print (occupation)
print (comment)
```

Comments in Python

Comments in your program code are lines of text that the interpreter ignores because they are written for humans to understand what a particular section of the code does. Comments in Python start with the hash sign (#). Anything that comes after this sign will be ignored by

```
#This is a comment. It will be ignored by the interpreter.
print ("Hello World!") #This is another comment
```

To write comments spanning multiple lines, you must start each line with the # symbol.

Multiple Statements on a Single Line

You can separate multiple lines written on a single line using a semi-colon. This rule only applies when neither of the statements on the line start a new block of code. Such a line would look like this:

```
name = "John"; age = 21;
```

Variables and Values

Variables and Assignment

You were taught in basic algebra that a variable represents a number. The same applies in Python, except that a variable can also represent other values besides numbers, which can be integers or floats (we will look at these briefly). In Exercise2, as an illustration, we took a variable "name" and assigned it a value "John". In Exercise3, we take another variable x and assign it a value 10.

Exercise3: Variable assignment

```
x = 10
print (x)
```

The statement x = 10 is what is called an assignment statement. Assignment is associating a value with a variable. In Python, the key to assignment statement is the use of an assignment operator which is the symbol =, as you know from math, the equal sign.

To put it in another way, the statement x = 10 binds a variable we named x to the value 10. In this case, x is a type **int** because it is bound to a value of integer type.

You can assign and re-assign a variable as often as wish. The variable type will change when you reassign it an expression of a different type.

The print statement in Exercise4.py displays the assigned value of variable x. Re-assigning the variable a different to the variable will evident after printing it.

Exercise4: Multiple variable assignment

```
x = 10
print (x)
x = "Apples"
print (x)
```

When you run exercise5.py, here is what you should see:

```
10
Apples
```

Exercise5: Assigning multiple variables same value

You can assign a single value to several variables simultaneously in Python. Consider this exercise:

```
x = y = z = 10
print (x)
```

```
print (y)
print (z)
```

When you run the script above, you will notice that the values of variables x, y, and z are all 10. This is because an integer object with the value 10 is created and all the variables are assigned to its memory location.

You can also assign multiple variables multiple values in one line of code. This is best illustrated in Exercise6.

Exercise6: Assigning multiple variables different values

```
name, age, occupation = "John", 21, "programmer"
print (name + age + occupation)
```

In Exercise6, three objects "John", 21, "programmer" are assigned to variables name, age, and occupation respectively.

Do not worry if the script prints *"John21programmer"* with no spaces—you get the point. The print statement in this exercise is for demonstration purposes. We will cover how to format your outputs later in the book.

Chapter 3. Basic Operators in Python

In programming, an operator is the construct which is used to manipulate the values of operands.

On your terminal, invoke the Python interpreter by typing Python then the following and press enter:

    5 + 9

    6 / 8

    90 * 21

You will notice that you can do these basic arithmetic calculations just by entering values separated by operands such as plus (+), minus (-), division (/), and multiplication (*).

Types of Operator

There are seven types of operators supported by the Python language. They are:

1.   Arithmetic operators

2.   Relational or Comparison operators.

3.   Assignment operators

4.   Logical operators

5.   Membership operators

6.   Identity operators

7.   Bitwise operators

Arithmetic Operators

Start your text editor and carry out Exercise7 to get some experience on how arithmetic operators in Python work.

Exercise7: Arithmetic Operators

```
x, y, z, f = 27, 10, -9, 4

a = x + y
print ("When you add x and y you get", a)

b = x - y
print ("When you subtract y from x you get", b)

c = x * y
print ("When you multiply x and y you get", c)

d = x / z
print ("When you divide x by z you get", d)

e = x % y
print (e, "is the remainder when x is divided by y")

g = x**f
print ("x to the power of 4 is", g)

h = x//y
print ("The floor division value of x divided by y is", h)
```

Here is a table summarizing the above (and more) arithmetic operators used in Python:

Operator	Description
+ Addition	Adds two values on either sides.
- Subtraction	Subtracts the value on the right side from that on the left.
* Multiplication	Multiplies values on either sides.
/ Division	Divides the value on the left side by that on the right.
% Modulus	Divides the value on the left by that on the right and returns the remainder.
** Exponent	Performs exponential (power) calculation of the value on the right by the value on the left.
// Floor Division	Divides the value on the left by that on the right and returns the quotient value of the result (without the decimal values).

Comparison Operators

As with the arithmetic operators, we will learn comparison by first writing a script then running it to see the results. Carry on with Exercise8.

Exercsie8.py: Comparison operators

```
x, y = 12, 10

if (x == y ):
   print ("1. x is equal to y")
else:
   print ("1. x is not equal to y")

if (x != y ):
   print ("2. x is not equal to y")
else:
   print ("2. x is equal to y")

if (x < y):
   print ("3. x is less than y")
else:
   print ("3. x is not less than y")
```

```
if (x > y):
    print ("4. x is greater than y")
else:
    print ("4. x is not greater than y")

if (x <= y):
    print ("5. x is either less than or equal to  y")
else:
    print ("5. x is neither less than nor equal to  y")

if (x >= y):
    print ("6. x is either greater than  or equal to y")
else:
    print ("6. x is neither greater than  nor equal to y")
```

Exercise8, demonstrates how to use relational operators. The table below summarizes what all the relational operators in Python do:

Operator	Description
==	Condition returns true if the value of the left and right operands are equal.
!=	Condition returns true if the value of the left and right operands are not equal.
>	Condition returns true if the value of the left operand is greater than the value of the right operand.
<	Condition returns true if the value of the left operand is less than the value of the right operand.
>=	Condition returns true if the value of the left operand is greater than or equal to the value of the right operand.
<=	Condition returns true if the value of the left operand is less than or equal to the value of right operand.

Assignment Operators

As the name suggests, assignment operators are used to assign values to variables. **Exercise9** demonstrates how these operators are used.

Exercise9: Assignment Operators

```
x, y, z = 12, 7, 0

z = x + y
print ("1. Value of z is ", z)

z += x
print ("2. Value of z is ", z)

z *= x
print ("3. Value of z is ", z)

z /= x
print ("4. Value of z is ", z)

z = 2
z %= x
print ("5. Value of z is ", z)

z **= x
print ("6. Value of z is ", z)

z //= x
print ("7. Value of z is ", z)
```

Here is a table that summarizes what each of the operators do.

Operator	Description
=	The equal signs assigns values on the right operand to that on the left side.

+= Add AND	Adds the value of the right operand to the value of the left operand then assign the result to left operand.
-= Subtract AND	Subtracts the value of the right operand from the value left operand then assigns the result to the left operand.
*= Multiply AND	Multiplies the value of the right operand with the value of the left operand then assigns the result to left operand.
/= Divide AND	Divides the value of the left operand by the value right operand then assigns the result to left operand.
%= Modulus AND	Takes the modulus using the values of the two operands then assigns the result to left operand.
**= Exponent AND	Performs exponential (power) calculation of the operators then assigns the result to the left operand.
//= Floor Division	It performs floor division on the operators then assigns the result to the left operand.

Other assignment operators you will come across at an advanced stage of learning Python are &=, |=, ^=, >>=, and <<=.

Logical Operators

There are three logical operators in Python: and, or, and not.

Exercise10: Logical operators

```
x = True
```

```
y = False

print ("When x is True and y is False:")

print ("x and y is", x and y)

print("x or y is", x or y)

print("not x is", not x)

print("not y is", not y)
```

Here is a summary of what the logical operators in Python do:

Operator	Meaning
and	Returns True if both the operands are True
or	Returns True if either of the operands is True
not	Returns True if operand is False and False if the operand is True.

Membership operators

There are two membership operators in Python: **in** and **not in**. They are used to test whether a variable or value is present in a sequence such as string, dictionary, list, set, or tuple. We will learn about these types later on.

Exercise11: Membership operators

```
x = "Hello World!"
y = {1:"x", 2:"y"}

print ("H" in x)

print ("Hello" not in x)
```

```
print (2 in y)

print ("z" in y)
```

The table below should help you understand why you get the result you see in Exercise11.

Operator	Meaning
in	Returns True if the variable or variable is found in the sequence.
not in	Returns True if the variable or value is not found in the sequence.

Identity operators

Identity operators are another kind of special operators in Python. They are is and is not. These operators are used to check if two variables or values are located on the same memory allocation.

Exercise12: Identity operators

```
x1 = 10
y1 = 10
x2 = "Hello"
y2 = "Hello"
x3 = [1, 2, 3]
y3 = [1, 2, 3]

print (x1 is not y1)
print (x2 is y2)
print (x3 is y3)
```

In this exercise, **x1** and **y1** are variables with similar values (integer value 10). This means that they are equal and identical, just as variables **x2** and **y2** with similar and equal string values. However, **x3** and **y3**, although equal, are not identical because they are lists and lists are mutable (this means they can be changed). The interpreter allocates the lists separate memory even when they are equal.

Here is a table defining what the identity operators do.

Operator	Meaning
is	Returns True if the operands are identical.
is not	Returns True if the operands are not identical.

Bitwise operators

Bitwise operators in Python act on operands in binary digit form, bit by bit. Here is a summary of the operations.

Operator	Meaning
&	Bitwise AND
|	Bitwise OR
~	Bitwise NOT
^	Bitwise XOR
>>	Bitwise right shift
<<	Bitwise left shift

Operator Precedence in Python

To evaluate expressions with more than a single operator, Python uses a rule of precedence that guides the order in which the operations are executed. For instance, multiplication has a higher precedence than addition, and addition higher than subtraction.

This rigid order can be changed using parentheses () as it has the highest precedence. The table below lists the precedence of all operators from the highest to the lowest.

	Operator	Description
1	()	Parentheses
2	**	Exponentiation (raise to the power)
3	~ + -	Complement, unary plus +@ and minus -@
4	* / % //	Multiply, divide, modulo and floor division
5	+ -	Addition and subtraction
6	>> <<	Right and left bitwise shift
7	&	Bitwise 'AND'
8	^ |	Bitwise exclusive `OR' and regular `OR'
9	<= < > >=	Comparison operators
10	<> == !=	Equality operators
11	= %= /= //= -= += *= **=	Assignment operators
12	Is, is not	Identity operators
13	In, not in	Membership operators
14	not, or, and	Logical operators

Chapter 4. Python Data Types I: Numbers and Strings

In Python, just as in any other object oriented programming language, every value has a (data) type. Everything in Python is an object and data types are considered classes while variables are the instances or objects of these classes.

The function **type()** is used to determine which class a particular value or variable belongs to and the **isinstance()** function is used to check whether an object belongs to a specific class. In this section, we are going to look at the most important data types and how to use them in basic programming.

Numbers

Integers, floating point, and complex, defined as **int, float**, and **complex** respectively, are the three classification of numbers in Python. A Number as a data type stores numeric values and is immutable, meaning that when the value of the variable is changed, a new object is allocated.

Creating number objects

Number objects (variables) are created when they are assigned values. In the following exercise, we will create three objects x, y, and z, when we assign them values.

Exercise13: Number Datatype

```
x = 7
print (x, "is of type", type(x))


y = 7.0
print (x, "is of type", type(x))


z = 1+2j
print ("is", z, "a complex number?", isinstance(1+2j,complex))
```

Unlike in most other OOP languages where the length of an integer is limited, in Python, an integer can be of any length and is only limited by the available memory in which it is stored.

A float, on the other hand, is accurate up to 15 decimal places. The difference between an integer and a float is a decimal point. For instance, in Exercise13, 7 is an integer while 7.0 is a floating point number.

Complex numbers in Python are written in the format **x + yj** where x is the real part of the number and y is the imaginary part. While it is good to know about them, complex numbers are not used much when programming in Python.

Deleting number objects

Reference to a number object can be deleted (removed from memory) using the statement **del**. The syntax of the **del** statement looks like this:

```
del x, y, z
```

You can delete a single object in one instance or multiple objects as in our example above.

Number Type Conversion

It is possible to convert numbers from one type to another in Python in a process that is also referred to as coercion. Operations such as multiplication, addition, subtraction, and division coerce integer numbers into floating point numbers implicitly if one of the operand is a float.

```
>>> 2 + 1.0
3.0
```

In this example, an integer (2) added to a float (1.0) gives the result as a float. To explicitly convert one number type to another, we use built-in functions **int()**, **float()** and **complex()** to coerce numbers to integers, floats, and complex types respectively. These functions can also convert strings with numeric values to the specified number types.

Exercise14.py: Number type coercion

```
x, y, z = 5.7, 10, "3.5j"

print (x, "is of type", type(x), y, "is of type", type(y), "and", z, "is a", type(z))

x = int(x); y = float(y); z = complex (z)

print ("After coercion, x new value is", x, ", y's new value is", y, "and z is of type", type(z))
```

As you can see in **Exercise14**, when a number is converted from a float to an integer, the number 5.7 is truncated to 5 and not rounded off (otherwise it would be 6).

Mathematical Functions

Python has in-built functions that can be used to perform mathematical calculations. The table below summarizes the description of each of the most common functions.

Function	(Description)
abs(x)	Returns the absolute value of x
ceil(x)	Returns the ceiling of x (the smallest integer that is not less than x)
cmp(x, y)	If x < y it returns -1, if x == y it returns 0, and if x > y it returns 1
exp(x)	Returns the exponential of x

fabs(x)	Returns the absolute value of x
floor(x)	Returns the floor value of x (the largest integer that is not greater than x)
log(x)	Returns the natural logarithm of x when x> 0
log10(x)	Returns the base -10 logarithm of x when x> 0
max(x1, x2,...)	Returns the highest value of the arguments
min(x1, x2,...)	Returns the lowest value of the arguments
modf(x)	Returns the fractional and integer parts of x as a tuple.
pow(x, y)	Returns the value of x**y.
round(x, [n])	Returns the value of x rounded to n digits from the decimal point.
sqrt(x)	Returns the square root of x when x > 0

Strings

A string is a sequence of characters enclosed in single ('), double ("), or triple (''' or """) quotes. It is among the most popular data types in Python. A string is created by simply enclosing Unicode (alphanumeric and symbolic) characters in quotes and assigning them to a variable. In Python, unlike most other OOP languages, single quotes are treated the same as double quotes.

Exercise15: Creating a string type

```
greeting = "Hello"
name = "John"
message = """This message is to show that you can have a
multi-line string when you use triple quotes.
The quotation marks can be single or double depending
on your preferences."""

print (greeting, name, message)
```

Strings are an immutable data type.

Accessing Values in a String

Because Python does not support a character type, each alphanumeric or symbolic character in a string is considered a substring of length one. We can use the slicing operator (square bracket [ ] to access the substrings and use an index that begins with 0 for the first substring to manipulate them.

Exercise16: Accessing values in a string

```
greeting = "Hello"
name = "John"
message = """This message is to show that you can have a
multi-line string when you use triple quotes.
The quotation marks can be single or double depending
on your preferences."""

print (greeting, name, message)
```

Slicing is best visualized by considering the index of each substring to be between the elements like this:

H	E	L	L	O		W	O	R	L	D	!	
0	1	2	3	4	5	6	7	8	9	10	11	12
-12	-11	-10	-9	-8	-7	-6	-5	-4	-3	-2	-1	

Updating Strings

The values in a string can be updated by re-assigning the variable to another string. The value of the new string may or may not be related to the previous values. Consider **Exercise17**.

Exercise17: Updating a string

```
greeting = "Hello World!"

print (greeting)

greeting = greeting[:6] + "John."

print ("Updated string = ", greeting)
```

What this exercise does is to "update" the string beginning at index 5 with the new string of characters.

Concatenating two or more strings

Concatenating is joining two or more string to make them one. In Python, we use the plus (+) operator to achieve this. You can use parentheses to concatenate strings in different lines and you can iterate through a string using the * operator as demonstrated in the next exercise.

Exercise18: Concatenation of strings.

```
greeting = "Hello!"
name1 = "John"
name2 = "World"
message = ("It's me "
    "again")

print (greeting + " " + name1)

print (greeting, name2)

print (greeting * 3, message)
```

The table below is a summary of the special string operators that you can use to manipulate and update substrings in a string, some of which we have already used in our exercises.

Operator	What it does

+ (Concatenation)	Combines values on either side of the operator.
* (Iteration)	Concatenates multiple copies of a string to create new strings.
[ ] (Slice)	Returns the character index from the given index
[:] (Range Slice)	Returns the substring characters from the given range
in (Membership)	Returns true if a character exists in the specified string
not in (Membership)	Returns true if a character does not exist in the specified string
r/R (Raw String)	Suppresses escape characters. The letter "r" or "R" precedes the first quotation marks.
% (Format)	Performs String formatting

Escape characters

If you use a single or double quotes to print a text like – "He asked, "What's that doing here?" – you will get a **SyntaxError: invalid syntax**. Try it, run the following line of code"

```
print ("He asked, "What's that doing here?"")
```

One way to get around such a problem is to use triple quotes. The other way is to use an escape sequence.

An escape sequence is the use of a backslash character to make the interpreter interpret a string differently. When you use a single quote to represent a string, all single quotes inside the string must be escaped and if you use double quotes, all the double quotes must be escaped. Here is how we would use an escape sequence to represent the above string:

```
print ("He asked, \"What's that doing here?\"")
print ('He asked, "What\'s that doing here?"')
```

Here is a table summarizing escape (or non-printable) characters that can be used with a backlash notation.

Backslash	Description
\a	Bell or alert
\b	Backspace
\cx	Control-x
\C-x	Control-x
\e	Escape
\f	Formfeed
\M-\C-x	Meta-Control-x
\n	Newline
\nnn	Octal notation, where n is in the range 0.7
\r	Carriage return
\s	Space
\t	Tab
\v	Vertical tab
\x	Character x
\xnn	Hexadecimal notation

String formatting with %

The format operator (%) is one of the best features in Python that is unique to strings. There is no better way to demonstrate how it works than in an example.

Exercise19: String formatting using %

print ("My name is %s and I am %d years old!" %("John", 21))

In this exercise, we formatted the string using a string placeholder %s and a decimal integer placeholder %d. Here is a table of all the symbols that can be used alongside % to format placeholders as used in Exercise19.

Format Symbol	Conversion
%c	character
%d	signed decimal integer
%i	signed decimal integer
%u	unsigned decimal integer
%f	floating point real number
%s	string conversion using str() before formatting
%e	exponential notation (with lowercase 'e')
%E	exponential notation (with UPPERcase 'E')
%x	hexadecimal integer (lowercase letters)
%X	hexadecimal integer (UPPERCASE letters)
%g	the shorter of %f and %e
%G	the shorter of %f and %E
%o	octal integer

Other symbols and functions supported by Python used to format strings are:

Symbol	Functionality
+	displays the sign
-	left justification

0	pad from left with zeroes (in place of spaces)
*	argument specifies width or precision
%	'%%' format with a single literal '%'
<sp>	Insert a blank space before a positive number
(var)	mapping variable (dictionary arguments)
#	Adds the octal leading zero ('0') or hexadecimal leading '0x' or '0X', when 'x' or 'X' is used.
m.n.	If applicable, m is the minimum total width and n is the number of digits to display after the decimal point.

String formatting with format()

A newer method of formatting strings is the use of the **format()** method. This method is both powerful and very versatile and is used with curly braces {} as placeholders for the fields or elements to be replaced. Positional arguments can be used to specify the order.

Exercise20: String formatting using format()

```
#Using default order
students1 = "{}, {} and {}".format("John","Mary","Bill")
print ("\nStudents by Default Order")
print (students1)

#Using positional argument
students2 = "{1}, {0} and {2}".format("John","Mary","Bill")
print ("\nStudents by Positional Order")
print (students2)

#Using keyword argument
students3 = "{m}, {b} and {j}".format(j="John", m="Mary", b="Bill")
print ("\nStudents by Keyword Order")
print (students3)
```

The **format()** method also has optional formatting specifications. They can be separated from the field name using a colon, the < operator can be used to justify the string to the left, ^ to the center, and > to the right within a given space. It can also be used to format integers as hexadecimal or binary etc. and floating point numbers can be formatted to round off or display in exponent format.

Other common string methods

There are many built-in methods that can be used with the string type of data in Python besides **format()**. Others common methods include **upper()**, **lower()**, **find()**, **replace()**, and **split()** just to name the most popular.

Exercise21: Practice with string methods

```
print ("Hello World!".lower())
print ("Hello World!".upper())
print (".split() splits words into a list".split())
print (["and", ".join", "joins", "a", "list", "into", "a", "string"])
print ("You can use .find to search for characters in a
string".find("search"))
print (".replace will replace a substring with
another".replace("replace","substitute"))
```

Chapter 5. Python Data Types II: Lists, Tuples, and Dictionary

Sequences are another basic type of data structure in Python. Each element in a sequence, be it a list, tuple, or dictionary, is assigned an index that marks its position. The first index is always zero, the second is one and so on. Python has six in-built types of sequences but the most common that every beginner should learn are lists and tuples.

Lists

A list is basically an ordered sequence of items. In Python, lists are among the most popular sequence data types because they are flexible (the items do not need to be of the same type), and declaring them is quite easy. Items in a list are enclosed within square brackets [ ] and are separated by commas.

Creating a list in Python

To create a list in Python, enclose items in square brackets separated by commas and assign it a variable.

Exercise22.py: Creating lists

```
weekdays = ["Monday", "Tuesday", "Wednesday", "Thursday", "Friday"]
yearlist = [2017, "Two Thousand and Seventeen", "XXVII", 20.17]
favorites = ["a", "x", "i", "xx"]

print (weekdays)
```

Just as in string indices, elements of a list are indexed starting at 0. They can be concatenated, sliced and so on.

Accessing values in a list

To access the values of a list, we use square bracket slicing and refer to the values using the index or indices. Try it out in **Exercise23**.

Exercise23: Accessing list values

```
months = ["Jan", "Feb", "Mar", "Apr", "May", "Jun", "Jul", "Aug", "Sep",
"Oct", "Nov", "Dec"]

print ("The first month is", months[0])
print ("The 5th to 9th months are", months[4:9])
print ("The second last month is", months[-2])
print (months[6:], "make up the last half of the year")
```

Updating a list

You can update a single element or multiple elements of a list simultaneously by specifying the slice on the left side of the assignment operator. Try it in the next exercise.

Exercise24: Updating a list

```
subjects = ["Math", "Physics", "Chemistry"]

print ("List of subjects:", subjects)

subjects[2] = "Biology"

print ("New list of subjects: ", subjects)
```

To add elements to a list, you use the **append()** function as in Exercise24.

Exercise25: Appending a new item to a list

```
subjects = ["Math", "Physics", "Chemistry"]

print ("List of subjects:", subjects)
```

```
subjects[2] = "Biology"

print ("New number of subjects: ", subjects)
```

Note that the **append()** function allows you to add only one item at a time.

Deleting an element in a list

There are two ways you can delete an element in a list. You can use the del statement if you know the exact element or elements you wish to delete or the remove() method if you do not. Let us put both these in practice in the next exercise.

Exercise26: Deleting an item in a list

```
subjects = ["Math", "Physics", "Chemistry", "Biology", "History"]

print ("List of subjects:", subjects)

del subjects[2]

print ("New list of subjects after del: ", subjects)

subjects.remove("Physics")

print ("New list of subjects after subjects.remove:", subjects)
```

Basic list operations

Just like strings, lists can be manipulated using operators such as + to concatenate and * to iterate. Generally speaking, lists respond to all the general sequence operations that we used on strings in the previous chapter. Try out the operations in Exercise27 to have a better grasp of what each does.

Exercise27: Basic lists operations

```
fruits = ["Mango", "Banana", "Orange", "Apple", "Pear"]
```

```
numbers1 = [1, 2, "three", 4]
numbers2 = [7, "x", "p", 10]

print ("The length of the fruits list is", len(fruits))

numbers = numbers1 + numbers2
print (numbers)
print (numbers1 * 2)
print (10 in numbers2)

for x in [1, 2, 3]: print (x)
```

The following table summarizes the built-in methods and functions that you can use to manipulate lists in Python:

Function	Description
cmp(list1, list2)	Compares the elements of two lists.
len(list)	Returns the total length of the list.
max(list)	Returns the item with max value from the list.
min(list)	Returns the item with min value from the list.
list(seq)	Converts a tuple into list.

The following list methods are built into Python:

Method	Description
list.append(x)	Appends an object x to list
list.count(x)	Returns the count of how many times x occurs in list
list.extend(seq)	Appends the contents of seq to list
list.index(x)	Returns the lowest index in list that x appears
list.insert(index, x)	Inserts object x into list at the specified index

list.pop(x=list[-1])	Removes and returns last object or x from list
list.remove(x)	Removes object x from list
list.reverse()	Reverses the list of objects
list.sort([func])	Sorts objects of list using compare func (if provided)

Tuples

Similar to list, a tuple is an ordered sequence of items. The only difference between it and a list is that a tuple is immutable. This means that once it has been created, it cannot be modified.

Tuples are used to create write-protected data. Because they are not dynamic, they are often faster than lists. A tuple is defined within parentheses () and the values are separated by commas. Like lists, a tuple can contain values of different data types.

    my_tuple = (5, "2017", 1+3j)

The slicing operator we used on strings and lists [] can be used to extract the items in a tuple, but values cannot be changed.

    tuple2 = (1, 2, 3, 4, 5)

An empty tuple is basically two parentheses with nothing between them

    empty_tuple = ()

To create a tuple with only one value, it must include a comma. Like this:

    Year = (2017,)

Just like strings and lists, the values within a tuples are references with indices that start at 0 and can be concatenated, sliced, and so on.

Accessing values in a tuple

Use the square bracket to slice along the index or indices and access the values of a tuple as in Exercise29.

Exercise29: Accessing values in a tuple

```
continents = ("Asia", "Africa", "Americas", "Europe", "Australia")
print ("continents[0]:", continents[0])
print ("continents[2:]", continents[2:])
print ("continents[:-3]", continents[:-3])
```

Updating a tuple

Tuples are immutable, which means that the tuple elements or values between the brackets cannot be changed or updated. However, you can take the values from an existing tuple and create a new tuple as demonstrated in Exercise30.

Exercise30: Updating a tuple

```
continents = ("Asia", "Africa", "Americas", "Europe", "Australia")
continents2 = ("Antarctica",)

all_continents = continents + continents2

print (all_continents)
```

Deleting tuple elements

It is not possible to remove individual values of a tuple. Therefore, the only option, as we saw with updating tuple values in Exercise30, is to create another tuple from the values of an existing tuple, discarding the undesired elements.

To delete an entire tuple, you can use the **del** statement. The syntax looks like this:

```
del tuple
```
Where tuple is the name of the tuple to delete.

Basic tuple operations

As we have already learned, tuples respond to most operators we used on strings and lists including + for concatenation and * for iteration. Generally speaking, tuples respond to all the operations we have used on strings. Therefore, we will not repeat them in this section. For your free practice time, find out which operations from strings and lists can be applied to tuples and find out what results they return.

Dictionaries

A dictionary in Python is an unordered collection of items separated by commas and enclosed in curly braces. Unlike other compound data types such as a list and a tuple which have only one value for an element, a dictionary has a pair of key and value separated by a colon. An empty dictionary without values will have empty curly braces.

The values of a dictionary may be any data type, but the data type of the keys must be immutable such as numbers, strings, or tuples. Dictionaries in Python are optimized to retrieve paired values using the element key.

Creating a dictionary

To create a dictionary, simply place item pairs separated by commas inside curly braces {}. Each item must have a key and a corresponding value in the format **key: value**.

Exercise31: Creating dictionaries

```
empty_dict = {}
integerkey_dict = {1: "Mango", 2: "Apple", 3: "Orange"}
```

```
mixedkey_dict = {"name": "John", 0: [2, 4, 3]}
print (integerkey_dict)
print (mixedkey_dict)
```

We can also create a dictionary using the built-in function **dict()**.

Accessing elements of a dictionary

While we used indexes to access the values of strings, tuples, and lists, with dictionaries, we use keys. To access an element in a dictionary, we use a key inside a square bracket or the **get()** method.

Exercise32: Accessing dictionary elements

```
my_dict = {"name":"John", "age": 21, "occupation":"Programmer"}
print (my_dict["name"])
print (my_dict.get('age'))
work = my_dict.get("occupation")
print (work)
```

If you use the square bracket method to access a key does not exist in the dictionary, it will return an **KeyError** but if you use the **get()** method it will return **None** instead.

Adding, deleting, and modifying elements in a dictionary

Because a dictionary is a mutable data type, you can add new or delete or update existing elements. If the key of the element you are changing exists, the value will get updated, else a new key: value pair will be created and added to the dictionary.

Exercise33: Deleting and updating dictionary elements

```
student = {"name": "John Doe", "age": 25, "grade": "B+"}
print ("Before update:", student)
print ("\nChange age to 30:\nAdd Sex key:value pair")
student["age"] = 30
```

```
student["sex"] = "Male"
print ("\nAfter update:", student)
print ("Delete grade entry:")
del student["grade"]
print ("After deleting grade:", student)
```

When you run Exercise33.py, you will learn that:

- You can update the value of a key in the dictionary by assigning it a new value using the traditional = operator.
- You can create a new **key:value** pair by assigning a non-existent key a new value as in student["sex"] = "Male".
- You can remove an individual dictionary element using the **del** operator.

You can also remove all the contents of a dictionary in a single operation using the **dict.clear()** method statement. You can also delete the entire dictionary by using **del dictionary** operation where dictionary is the name of the dictionary.

Here is a table summarizing the built-in methods and functions you can use to manipulate a dictionary in Python.

Function	Description
cmp(dict1, dict2)	Compares the elements of dict1 to those of dict2.
len(dict)	Returns the total length of the dictionary (the number of items in the dictionary)
str(dict)	Returns a printable string representation of the dictionary
type(variable)	Returns the type of the passed variable.

The next table is a presentation of the methods that you can use to manipulate the elements of a dictionary:

Methods	Description
dict.clear()	Removes all the elements of the dictionary dict
dict.copy()	Returns a shallow copy of the dictionary dict
dict.fromkeys()	Creates a new dictionary with keys from seq with values set to value.
dict.get(x, default=None)	Returns the value of key x in the dict dictionary or default if the does not exist.
dict.has_key(x)	Returns True if key x is in dictionary dict, otherwise False
dict.items()	Returns a list of dict's (key, value) pairs in tuple format.
dict.keys()	Returns list of keys of the dict dictionary.
dict.setdefault(x, default=None)	Returns the value of key x in the dict dictionary or set dict[key]=default if key does not exist.
dict.update(dict2)	Adds dictionary key:value pairs from dict to dict
dict.values()	Returns a list of values from the dict dictionary.

Properties of dictionary keys

While the values of a dictionary in Python have no restriction – they can be made up of any arbitrary objects or data types, which include standard or user-defined objects – keys are different. There are two vital points you must know about dictionary keys in Python:

1.   You cannot enter more than one key in a dictionary. This means you cannot have duplicate keys in a single dictionary.

2.   Unlike values, keys are immutable. This means you can use types such as strings, tuples, and strings as keys, but you cannot define a key using something like ["Key").

Chapter 6: Decision Making in Python

Decisions are a core part of programming. Because we will always create programs that anticipate certain conditions to be met during normal execution, as programmers, we must specify actions that the program should take when the conditions are met.

What decision structures do is to evaluate one or multiple expressions which return **TRUE** or **FALSE** outcomes. We can then determine what actions the program should take by defining the statements to execute when the outcome is **TRUE** or **FALSE**.

The if statement

The diagram below is a flowchart diagram of a basic decision making structure used in most programming languages.

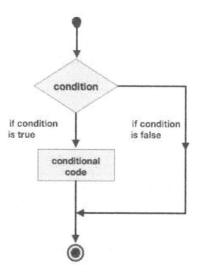

In Python, any **non-null** and **non-zero** value returned is regarded as **TRUE** while a **null** or **zero** value is assumed to be **FALSE**. The decision making structure demonstrated in the figure above represents the most basic conditional statement that uses the **if** statement that we first used in *Exercise8.py*.

Here is the syntax of the **if** decision making structure:

```
if condition_test:
    statement
```
Note: Indentation is very important.

Exercise34: if statement

```
x = 10
if x == 10:
    print ("x = 10")
```

What this simple exercise does is this:

1. First, the variable x is created and assigned a value of 10.
2. The decision making structure if evaluates whether the value of x is equal to 10.
3. The string "x = 10" is displayed on the screen should the **if** statement evaluate to TRUE.

Note that we can also write the **if** statement in this format:

```
x = 10
if x == 10: print ("x = 10")
```

The if... else statement

So far, we have seen that we can use the **if** statement to evaluate condition and execute a statement when the results evaluates to TRUE. However, with the **if** statement, nothing happens when the condition evaluates to FALSE.

With the **if... else** statement, we can provide an alternative statement for the interpreter to execute should the condition being evaluated evaluate to

FALSE. Here is the flowchart diagram of the if… else structure of decision making in Python:

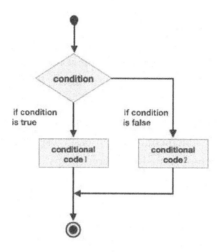

In **Exercise8**, we wrote a program that evaluates whether one variable is equal to another and to execute a statement if it is, or execute a second if it is not. We used the if… else condition to achieve this.

The syntax of an **if… else** statement takes this format:

```
if condition_test:
    statement_of_if
else:
    statement_of_else
```

Exercise35: if… else condition

```
x, y = 12, 12

if (x == y ):
    print ("x is equal to y")
else:
    print ("x is not equal to y")
```

Can you change the values of the variables x or y to make them equal and see what happens when you run the script?

if...elif...else statement

The **if... else** statement is a way for the program to evaluate a condition, and execute a statement when the condition returns TRUE or execute another when it returns FALSE. With Python, you can evaluate a condition more than once and use the **if... else** statement more than once. However, rather than use an **else... if** statement, you can easily use elif. **elif** is the short of **else if**. This is best demonstrated in Exercise36.py.

Exercise36.py: Nested if statements

```
age = int(input("Enter age to evaluate:"))

if age >= 18:
    agegroup = "Adult"

elif age >= 13:
    agegroup = "Teenager"

elif age >=0:
    agegroup = "Child"

else:
    agegroup = "Invalid"

print (agegroup)
```

In Exercise36, the program prompts the user to enter an integer to evaluate. It checks whether the input is equal to or greater than 18 and if **TRUE**, determines that the agegroup is Adult. If it is not equal or greater than 18, which means the condition returns **FALSE**, it moves on to the next elif block for evaluation and so on. At the end, there is an else statement that is executed should all the elif statements return **FALSE**.

The flowchart diagram of the **if... elif... else** construct looks like this:

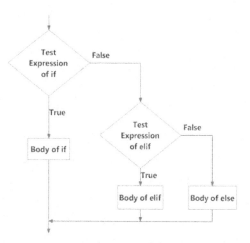

Nested if statement

With Python, you can use one **if** or **if... elif... else** statement inside another **if... elif... else** statement or statements. This forms a nested structure of **if** and **if... else**'s. The only way to figure out which level of nesting a statement is at before arriving at the last else statement is by using indentation. Because nesting if statements can be very confusing, you should try to avoid using it if you can.

Exercise37 illustrates how a nested if... elif... else statement looks like.

Exercise37: Nested if statement

```
number = float(input("Enter a number to evaluate: "))

if number >= 0:
    if number == 0:
        print (number, "is a Zero")
    else:
        print (number, "is a positive number")
else:
    print (number, "is a negative number")
```

Chapter 7: Loops in Python

Statements in a program you write are typically executed sequentially: The first line of your code is executed first, followed by the second and then the third and so on. However, there may arise a situation where you need a line or a block of code to be executed severally.

Python offers a number of control structures that you can make your program follow complicated execution paths, typically by repeating a line or a block of code until a particular condition is met. This iteration or repetition of code is referred to as looping in programming and we use a loop statement to execute one or more statements multiple times.

The following flowchart diagram illustrates how a loop statement works:

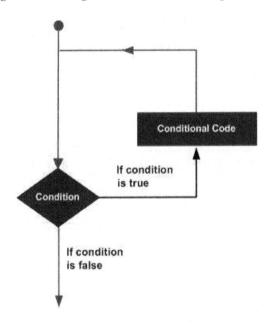

In Python, there are three ways you can create a loop or loops in your code. They include:

1. **for loop**: The **for** statement is used to execute a sequence of statements multiple times and abbreviate the program code that handles the loop variable.
2. **while** loop: The **while** statement is used to iterate one or a group of statements for as long as a given condition evaluates to TRUE. This type of loop tests a condition before the loop body is executed. A variation of this loop is **do... while**.
3. Nested loop: A nested loop is created when you use one or more loop(s) inside **for, while**, or **do... while** loop.

The for Loop

We use a loop that begins with the statement **for** in Python to iterate sequences such as lists, tuples, and strings, and other iterable objects. The process by which a sequence is iterated is called **traversal**.

Syntax of for Loop

The syntax of the for loop looks like this:

```
for value in sequence:
    body_of_for
```

The value in the syntax is the value of the variable inside the sequence on the current iteration. The loop will continue until the value reaches the last item in the sequence. The **body_of_for** is the statement of the loop that is separated from the rest of the code by indentation.

To make it easier to understand, below is a simplified flowchart figure of a for loop

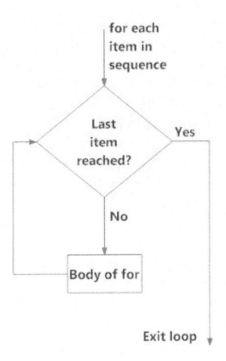

Exercise38: The for loop

This Program finds the sum of all the numbers in a list

```
numbers = [3, 9, 16, 7, 8, 2, 5, 4, 10] #List of numbers
sum = 0 #variable to store the sum
for val in numbers: #iterate over the list
    sum = sum + val
print ("The sum is", sum)
```

The range() function

The **range()** function can be used to generate a sequence of numbers. For instance **range(10)** will generate a list of 10 numbers between 0 and 9. Note that this function does not store the values it generates in memory.

You can use **start, stop,** and **step size** to define the parameters of the numbers to generate on the go or leave out the parameters to use the defaults which is 1. You can also use the **list()** function to force the **range()** function to output all items

The syntax for the **range()** with parameters defined is:

```
range(<start>, <stop>, <step size>)
```

Exercise39: The range() function with for loop

```
total = 0

for x in range(10,20,2):
    total = total + x
    print (x, "\n")

print ("The totals is:", total)
```

for... else loop

Just as we learnt in the previous chapter that the **if** decision making structure can have an else block, the **for** loop can have the else part as well. With this iteration structure, the else part is executed if the items in the sequence defined in the **for** loop are exhausted.

Later on in this chapter, we will learn about the break statement which is used to stop a loop. When the break statement is used in the for loop, the else block will be ignored. This means that the else part of the for loop will only run if no break of the loop occurs.

Exercise40: for... else loop

```
numbers = [0, 1, 3, 5, 6, 9, 10]

for i in numbers:
    print (i)
else:
    print("No more numbers to print.")
```

In this script, the **for** loop will print the value of i while iterating through the list until the loop is exhausted. At this point, the else block will be executed.

while loop

In Python, the while loop tests a condition (an expression) and as long as it returns **TRUE**, a block of code will be executed. This loop is used when the number of times the block of code will be iterated before the condition tests **FALSE** is not known beforehand.

Syntax of while loop

The syntax of the while loop takes this form:

```
while test_expression:
    body_of_while
```

In the code syntax above, the test expression will be checked first. The interpreter will only enter the body of the while loop only if the test expression evaluates to **TRUE**. The test expression will be checked again after one iteration and the process continues until such time that the test expression evaluates to **FALSE**.

As with the previous for loop, the body of the while loop is identified by its indentation. The first unindented line of code after the body_of_while marks the end of the while loop.

Python will identify any **non-zero** value returned when it tests the while expression as **TRUE** and **zero** and **None** values as **FALSE**.

Below is a flow chart of a while loop.

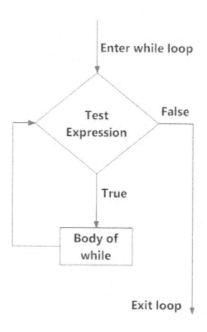

Enter while loop

Exercise41: While loop

```
x = int(input("Enter a value for x: "))

sum = 0
i = 1

while i <= x:
    sum = sum + i
    print (sum)
    i = i + 1   # update counter
print ("The total sum is", sum)
```

Our script in **Exercise41** adds natural numbers up to the number it prompts the user to enter. The test condition will evaluate to **TRUE** for as long as the counter (variable i) is less than or equal to the value of x that the user enters.

Note that we must increase the value of the counter variable in the body of the while loop. This is very important to prevent an infinite (never-ending) loop that could almost certainly cause the computer to freeze.

While... else loop

Just as we saw in the **for** loop in the previous sub-chapter, with the while loop, we can have an optional **else** block. The **else** part of the loop is executed only when the condition in the while test evaluates to false. Also, as with the **for** loop, when we use a break statement, the **else** block is skipped and the loop is terminated. Let us try out how the else block works in *Exercise42.py*.

Exercise42: While... else loop

```
loops = int(input("Enter the number of times to loop: "))

counter = 0

while counter < loops:
    counter = counter + 1
    print ("Iterations so far:", counter)

else:
    print("Maximum loops of", loops, "reached")
```

In this exercise, we use a counter variable to print the number of loops until the maximum the user sets using the variable loops. When the maximum number of loops is reached, the else statement is executed which is a string of the maximum loops reached.

Loop Control Statements

The **break, continue,** and **pass** statements in Python can be used to alter the flow of a normal loop, altering the sequence of statement execution. Simply put, these statements are used to terminate an iteration without checking the test condition. When execution leaves a loop, all objects created in the loop are destroyed.

The break statement

The break statement terminates the loop containing it and causes the statement immediately following the body of the loop to be executed next. If the break statement is used inside a nested loop, it will only terminate the innermost loop.

The syntax of break is just the word **break**. In a flow chart, the break statement takes this structure:

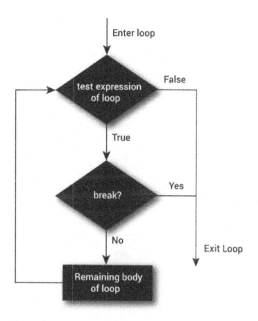

Exercise43: break statement

```
for val in "Hello World!":
    if val == "r":
        break
    print (val)

print ("Search letter 'r' found!")
```

In this exercise, we iterate though the string sequence "Hello World!", the condition being checking if the current character is "r" after which the current letter is printed. When we find "r", the loop breaks and terminates. The statement immediately following the body of the loop is executed.

The continue statement

The continue statement is used to skip the remainder of the code within the loop body for the current iteration only. Unlike break, continue does not terminate the loop; the test condition will be rechecked again prior to reiteration.

The syntax of the continue statement is the word **continue**. When presented in a flowchart, the continue structure looks like this:

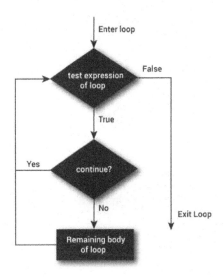

Exercise44: continue statement

```
for val in "Hello World!":
    if val == "r":
        continue
    print (val)
```

```
print ("Search letter 'r' found!")
```

Exercise44.py is a lot like the previous exercise, except that we use continue in place of break. Do you notice the difference in the output result?

The pass statement

In Python, when a statement is syntactically required in the code but you do not want it executed, you can use the pass statement to have it skipped. We can say that pass is a null statement or a placeholder for future implementation of a line or block of code such as in loops or functions.

Pass is different from a comment that is marked with #. While the interpreter completely ignores a comment, the pass statement is not ignored; it just is not executed. It results in no operation (NOP). The syntax for pass is the word **pass**.

When the pass statement is used in an empty class or function, it looks like this:

```
class My_Class:
    pass

def function(args):
    pass
```

Chapter 8. Input, Output, Files and Import

In this chapter, we are going to focus on two in-built functions in Python that we have used throughout the book so far: the **print()** function that displays text on the screen and the **input()** function that captures a user's input via the keyboard. We will also look at how to use **import** to call in-built modules to use in our programs.

Output Using the print() function

You are probably already familiar with the **print()** function because we have used it in almost every exercise we have carried out so far. This function is used to output data to the standard output device, which in our case, is the computer screen. We can also print to a file (we will cover this later in this chapter).

So far, we know that the syntax of the print function is print (). The actual syntax of this function is:

Print (*objects, sep=' ', end='\n', file=sys.stdout, flush=False)

In this statement:

- **objects** refers to the value or values to be printed.
- **sep** refers to the separator used between the values which is a space character by default.
- **end** is printed after all the values are printed. This is a new line by default.
- **file** is the default object where the values are printed. **sys.stdout** is the computer screen.
- **flush** writes out any data lingering in the program buffer to the standard output file.

Let us test out these parameters in a simple exercise.

Exercise45: The print() function parameters

```
print (1, 2, 3, 4, 5)
print (1,2,3,4, sep = '*')
print (1,2,3,4, sep = '#', end='&')
```

Notice how the new parameters affect the output of the **print()** function? It is good to know!

Exercise46: The print() function

```
name = "John"
print ("1. My name is" + name)
print ("2. My name is", name)
```

When you run the script above, you will notice that the **print()** function adds a space between the string and the variable name when separated by a comma in the second output. When we use a + operator to combine the string and variable, no space is added.

Output formatting

Sometimes you may want to format your program output to add some aesthetic value or to meet your program's requirements. You can achieve this using the **str.format()** method which is visible to any string object.

Exercise47: str.format()

```
name = "John"
age = 21

print ("My name is {} and I am {} years old.".format(name,age))
```

The curly braces ({}) in this exercise are used as placeholders. It also possible to specify the order in which the formatted characters are printed using tuple index numbers. Let us try it in Exercise48.

Exercise48: String formatting with placeholders

```
print ("My name is {0} and I am {1} years old.".format("John", 21))
print ("I am a {1} year old programmer named {0}.".format("John", 21))
```

We can even go a step further and use keyword arguments in formatting a string output as in Exercise49.

Exercise49: String formatting with arguments

```
print   ("Hello.   My   name   is   {name},   and   I   am   a
{occupation}.".format(occupation = "programmer", name = "John"))
```

Input

Most of the exercises we have done so far have had static variables, meaning that the values of the variables were hard coded in the source code of the programs. In a few of them, we have asked the user to enter an integer value which we assigned a variable.

In Python, we use the **input()** function to prompt the user to enter a value. The syntax looks like this:

```
Input ("The prompt to be displayed on screen: ")
```

The string "The prompt to be displayed on screen:" is optional.

Once the user enters data, we can then use the data conversion methods we learnt in chapters 4 and 5 to convert it into the type we can use.

Exercise50: input and output

Let us bring together a couple of things we have learnt so far into one exercise.

```
name = str(input("Enter your name: "))
age = int(input("How old are you?: "))
sex = str(input("Enter your gender M or F: "))
```

```
location = str(input("Which city do you live in: "))

if sex == "M" or "m":
    gender = "male"
elif sex == "F" or "f":
    gender = "female"
else:
    gender = "invalid"

print ("{}, you are a {} old {} from {}.".format(name, age, gender,
location))
```

Python File Input and Output

In modern computing, a file is a named location on a disk where related information is stored. The data is stored permanently in a non-volatile memory such as a hard disk drive or a flash memory disk.

The computer volatile storage memory known as the Random Access Memory (RAM) stores data temporarily. This means that the information is lost when power to the storage location is lost such as when the computer is turned off.

When we want to read, we must first open it by loading into the RAM and when we are done making changes, we must save it to the permanent memory to preserve its contents. In Python, this operation is executed in this three-step order:

1. The file is opened.
2. The file is read and/or written into.
3. The file is closed.

When a file is closed, the resources tied to it are freed.

Opening a file

Python has a built-in **open()** function that is used to open a file from the permanent memory. When used, this function returns a file object called a handle that can be used to read or modify the file contents.

The syntax to open a text file named poem would look like this:

```
f = open("poem.txt")   #to open a file in current directory
f = open(poem.txt, "r",) #to open a file in current directory for reading
f = open("C:/Python33/poem.txt")  #to specify full path
```

We can also specify the mode in which we want to open a file. The mode is basically a specification whether to open the file in read ('r'), write ('w'), or append ('a') file modes.

The default mode is read in text mode which reads the contents of the file as strings. When working with non-text files such as executable (.exe) and image files, you can specify binary mode to return content in byte form.

Exercise51: Opening a text file

If you downloaded the bonus archive with .py files thast comes with this book, there should be a text file named poem.txt in your working directory. If not, create a text file named poem.txt to use in this exercise.

```
f = open("poem.txt", "r")
poem = f.read(96);

print (poem)
```

In this exercise, the script opens the text file named poem.txt in read only mode, and assigns the first 96 string characters of the file to a variable called poem. We use the print() method to display what our program has read.

The table below summarizes the file modes you can specify when opening a file and what they mean.

Mode	Description
'r'	This is the default open mode. It opens a file for reading.
'w'	Opens a file for writing. Truncates the file if it exists or creates a new one if it does not.
'x'	Opens a file for exclusive creation. The operation fails if the file already exists.
'a'	Opens for appending at the end without truncation. Creates a new file if it does not exist.
't'	This is the default mode. It opens file in text mode.
'b'	Opens file in binary mode.
'+'	Opens a file for updating (enables reading and writing)
rb	Opens a file as read-only in binary format.
r+	Opens a file for reading and writing and places the file pointer at the beginning of the file
rb+	Opens a file for reading and writing in binary format, the pointer placed at the beginning of the file.
wb	Opens a file for writing only in binary format
w+	Opens a file for writing and reading. If file already exists, it is overwritten. If it does not, a new file is created for reading and writing.
wb+	Opens a file for writing and reading in binary format. If file already exists, it is overwritten. If it does not, a new file is created for reading and writing.

ab	Opens a file for appending in binary format. The file pointer is positioned at the end of the file if the file exists. If the file does not, a new file is created for writing.
a+	Opens a file for appending and reading, the file pointer positioned at the end of the file. If the file does not, a new file is created for reading and writing.
ab+	Opens a file for appending and reading in binary format, the file pointer positioned at the end of the file. If the file does not, a new file is created for reading and writing.

Writing to a File

To enable writing on to a file, you must open an existing file in write 'w', append 'a', or in exclusive creation 'x' modes. You must be careful when opening an existing file in 'w' mode because it will overwrite the existing file content, erasing everything that was previously in it.

To write a string of text or a sequence of bytes (when working with a binary file), you will use the **write()** method. Using this method returns the number of characters written on to the file. The syntax for the write() method looks like this:

```
file.write(string);
```
Exercise52: Writing to a file

```
file = open("myfile.txt", "w")
file.write("The purple cow poem is a short nonsense poem first published
in 1895 written by American writer Gelett Burgess");

file.close()

text = open("myfile.txt", "r+")
mytext = text.read(120);
```

print (mytext)

file.close()

In exercise52, we open a file named myfile.txt in write mode. However, because the file does not exist in the directory, one is created. We then write a string of text and close the file using the close() method. The statements below close are meant to show that we have indeed created the file and saved text in it, which we then display on the screen using the print() method.

Exercise53: Writing multiple lines of string to file

```
with open ("test.txt", "w", encoding = "utf-8") as file:
    file.write ("This is a unique file called test.txt\n")
    file.write ("We can choose to add a second line of text\n")
    file.write ("Or go all out and add another one\n")
```

Exercise53 creates a new file named test.txt using the utf-8 encoding. If a file called textfile.txt exists in the directory we are working on, it will be overwritten. We then use the **write()** method to write strings of text into it.

Reading From a File

We must open an existing file in reading mode to be able to read its contents.

There are several ways we can achieve this, some of which we have used in the previous exercises already. We can use the read(size) method to specify the amount of data to read or leave the brackets empty to let the method read to the end of the file and return the string of text.

We can also change the current file position using the seek() method or the tell() method to return the current position of the cursor (in bytes). The syntaxes of these methods look like these:

```
file.tell() #This returns the position of the current file.
File.seek(0) #This method brings the cursor to the start of the file.
```

Can you practice using these methods on the text files we have created so far? You can use these methods with the print() method to print out the result. For instance, your syntax will look like this:

```
text.tell()
print(text.read(96))
```

Closing a file

When you are done manipulating the contents of a file, you must properly close it to release the computer's memory resources. Remember that a file is loaded to the primary memory (RAM) when it is opened, and although Python has an in-built garbage collector that cleans up unreferenced objects periodically, your program should not rely on it to close files no longer in use.

Opened and created files are closed using the method **close()**. The syntax looks like this:

```
file = open("test.txt",encoding = 'utf-8')
# Manipulate the contents of your file here. Remember to save them.
file.close()
```

This method of closing a file is completely safe. However, in some cases, errors such as encoding type may cause an exception when the file is closing, resulting in code existing on memory without the file being properly closed. At advanced levels of studying Python, you will discover a try... finally structure of handling exceptions that deals with such issues. The code would look like this:

```
try:
    file = open("test.txt",encoding = 'utf-8')
    # Manipulate the contents of your file here. Remember to save them.
finally:
    file.close()
```

Python File Methods

There are a number of methods in Python that you can use with the file object. We have used some of them already in previous exercises. The table below is a presentation of the rest of the methods you should use when practicing with text files.

Method	Description
tell()	Returns the current file location.
fileno()	Returns an integer number of the file descriptor.
read(x)	Reads at most 'x' characters form the file. If x is not defined or negative, reads till end of file.
writable()	Returns TRUE if the file stream can be written to.
close()	Closes an open file. If the file is already closed, it has no effect.
seek(offset,from=S EEK_SET)	Changes the file position to 'offset' bytes, in reference to 'from' (start, current, end).
write(x)	Writes string 'x' to the file then returns the number of characters written.
writelines(lines)	Writes a list of lines to the file.
seekable()	Returns TRUE if the file stream supports random access.
detach()	Separates and returns the underlying binary buffer from the TextIOBase.
isatty()	Returns TRUE if the file has an interactive stream.
readable()	Returns TRUE if the file stream can be read.
truncate(size=Non e)	Resizes the file stream to defined size in bytes. If the size is not specified, it resizes to current location.

flush()	Flushes the file stream write buffer.
readline(x=-1)	Reads and returns one line from the file or if specified, at most x bytes.
readlines(x=-1)	Reads and returns a list of lines from the file. Returns at most x bytes or characters if x is specified.

Importing Modules

When you begin gaining more experience and learning even more practical lessons on programming using Python, you will begin creating bigger and more complex programs. With time, you will find it necessary to break these scripts into different modules.

A module is a file that contains the definitions and statements that your program needs. Python modules have a filename with an extension .py, just like the scripts you have been creating in exercises in this book.

Definitions contained inside a module can be imported and used in another module or called by the interactive Python interpreter. We use the import keyword to achieve this. Let us try it in the next exercise.

Exercise54: Importing Modules

```
import math

print (math.pi)
```

When you run the above script, it will display the value of pi on the screen. This is because Python has imported the math module, which contains pi.

We can also import specific attributes and functions rather than the entire module. TO achieve this, we use the **from** keyword. Here is an example.

```
from math import pi

print (pi)
```

When you use the import keyword to import modules, functions, or attributes of a module, Python looks at several locations defined in sys.path. You can check these locations using by importing the sys module then typing sys.path, like this:

```
import sys
sys.path
```

When you become a seasoned Python developer, you will be able to add your own locations to the sys.path locations as well.

Chapter 9. Functions and Arguments

A function is a block of related statements that performs a single but very specific task. Functions are used to provide modularity to complex applications and are defined to be re-usable. Functions such as **print()** and **import()** are examples of built-in functions that come with the development platform.

Python allows you to create your own functions that go a long way to help you break your program into smaller chunks. As you create complex applications, you will find it necessary to create functions that will not only make your applications more organized and manageable but also save you time in the future because you will have chunks of reusable code saved away.

Syntax of a Function

The syntax of a function looks like this:

```
def function_name(parameters):
    """"docstring"""
    statement(s)
    return [expression]
```

Here is a breakdown of what the syntax of a function:

- **def** keyword: This marks the beginning of the function header.
- **function_name**: This is a unique name that identifies the function. The rules of the function name are almost similar to those of a variable we learnt at the beginning of this book.
- **parameters** or **arguments**: Values are passed to the function by enclosing them in parentheses (). Parameters are optional.
- The colon marks the end of the function header.

- **"""docstring"""**: (Docstring) is an optional documentation string. It describes the purpose of the function.
- **statement(s)**:There must be one or more valid statements that make up the body of the function. Notice that the statements are indented (typically tab or four spaces).
- There may be an optional return statement that returns a value or values from the function.

Creating and calling a function

To use a function you create in your script, you will need to call it from the Python prompt, program, or function.

Exercise55: Creating a function

```
def greeting(name):
    """This function greets the user when
    the person's name is passed in as
    a parameter"""
    print ("Greetings,", name + "!")
```

You can call a function by simply typing its name along with the appropriate parameters.

Modify the previous Exercise55 code to see how you can call the function greeting.

Exercise56: Calling a function

```
def greeting(name):
    """This function greets the user when
    the person's name is passed in as
    a parameter"""
```

```
print ("Greetings,", name + "!")

username = str(input("Enter your name: "))
greeting(username)
```

The code in Exercise55 first defines a function called greeting, which requires one argument, name. It will prompt the user to enter a string, which will be assigned the variable username and used as the argument when the function greeting is called.

Docstring

The first string of text immediately after the function header is called the documentation string, or in short, docstring. This section of the function is optional and briefly explains what the function does. It is a good practice to include a descriptive docstring whenever you create a new function because you, or another programmer going through your code at a later time, may need it to understand what the function does. Always document your code!

We have exhaustively explained what our greeting function does. As you can see, we used a triple quote string to make it possible for the description to extend to multiple lines. Within the attribute of the function, the docstring is available as **__doc__**.

For instance, the greeting function would appear in the Python shell print() function output as in Exercise57.

Exercise57: Printing the docstring

```
def greeting(name):
    """This function greets the user when
    the person's name is passed in as
    an argument."""
```

```
print ("Greetings,", name + "!")
```

```
print (greeting.__doc__)
```

The return statement

The optional return statement in a function is used as an exit to return execution back to where from it was called. The syntax of the return statement as we have seen takes this form:

```
return [expression_list]
```

The return statement may contain expressions that get evaluated to return a value. If there is no expression in the statement or when the **return** statement is not included in the function, the defined function will return a **None** object when called. Our greeting function in Exercises 55 through 57 return a value of **None** because we have not included a return statement.

Exercise58: The return statement

```
def agegroup_checker(age):
    """This function returns the
    user's age group name based
    on the age entered."""

    if age >= 18:
        agegroup = "Adult"

    elif age >= 13:
```

```python
        agegroup = "Teenager"

    elif age >=0:
        agegroup = "Child"

    else:
        agegroup = "Invalid"

    return (agegroup)

age = int(input("Enter your age to check age group:"))
print ("Your age group is:", agegroup_checker(age))
```

Function Arguments

In Python, you can call a function using any of these four types of formal arguments:

- Default arguments.
- Required arguments
- Keyword arguments
- Variable-length arguments

Default arguments

A default argument assumes the default value if no value is specified within the function's call parameters.

Exercise59: Default arguments

```
def studentinfo(name, gender = "Male"):
  "This function prints info passed in the function parameters."
  print ("Name:", name)
  print ("Gender:", gender)
  return;


studentinfo ( name = "John")
studentinfo ( name = "Mary", gender = "Female")
```

In Exercise59, you can see how we have specified the default value for the parameter gender as "Male". When we do not define the gender within one of the values, the default value is used.

Required arguments

Required arguments must be passed to the function in the exact positional order to match the function definition. If the arguments are not passed in the right order, or if the arguments passed are more or less than the number defined in the function, a syntax error will be encountered.

Keyword arguments

Functions calls are related to keyword arguments. This means that when a keyword argument is used in a function call, the caller should identify the argument by the parameter name. With these arguments, you can place arguments out of order or even skip the entirely because the Python interpreter will be able to match the values provided with the keywords provided.

Exercise60: Keyword arguments

```
def studentinfo(name, age):
```

```
"This function prints info passed in the function parameters."
print ("Name:", name, "Age:", age)
return;


studentinfo (age = 21, name = "John")
```

Note that with keyword arguments in Exercise60, the order of the parameters does not matter.

Variable-length arguments

In some cases, a function may need to process more arguments than the number you specified when you defined it. These variables are known as variable-length arguments. Unlike required and default arguments, variable-length arguments can be included in the definition of the function without being assigned a name.

The syntax for a function with non-keyword variable-length arguments takes this format:

```
def studentinfo(name, age):
    "This function prints info passed in the function parameters."
    print ("Name:", name, "Age:", age)
    return;


studentinfo (age = 21, name = "John")
```

Notice that an asterisk is placed right before the tuple name that holds the values of non-keyword variable arguments. If no additional arguments are defined when the function is called, the tuple will remain empty.

10. Objects and Class

We have already learnt that Python is an object oriented programming language. There are other languages that are procedure oriented that emphasize on functions, but in Python, the stress is on objects. But then, what is an object?

Simply put, an object is a collection of methods (functions) that act on data (variables) which are also objects. The blueprint for these objects is a class.

Consider a class a sketch or a prototype that has all the details about an object. If your program were a car, a class would contain all the details about the design, the chassis, where tires are, and what the windshield is made of. It would be impossible to build a car without a class defining it. The car is the object.

Because many cars can be built based on the prototype, we can create many objects from a class. We can also call an object an instance of a class, and the process by which it is created is called **instantiation**.

Defining a Class

Classes are defined using the keyword **class**. Just like a function, a class should have a documentation string (docstring) which briefly explains what the class is and what it does. While the docstring is not mandatory, it is a good practice to have it. Here is a simple definition of a class called **NewClass**:

```
class NewClass:

    """This is the docstring of the class NewClass that we

    Just created. Our program now has a new class"""

    pass
```

When you create a new class, a new local namespace that defines all its attributes is created. Attributes in this case may include functions and data structures. In it, it will contain special attributes that start with __ (double underscores) e.g. __doc__ that defines the docstring of the class.

When a class is defined, a new class object with the same name is created. The new class object is what we can use to access the different attributes and to instantiate the new objects of our new class.

Exercise61: Creating a new class

```
class NewClass:
    """This is our first class. What it does
    is display a string text and a value of
    variable name"""
    name = str(input("Enter your name: "))
    def greeting (name):
        print ("Hello", name)


print (NewClass.name)
print (NewClass.greeting)
print (NewClass.__doc__)
```

What does your console display when you run the script in Exercise61?

Creating an Object

So far, we have learnt that we can access the different attributes of a class using the class objects. We can use these objects to also instantiate new instances of that class using a procedure a lot similar to calling a function.

MyObject = NewClass()

In the example above, a new instance object called **MyObject** is created. This object can be used to access the attributes of the class **NewClass** using the class name as a prefix.

The attributes in this case may include methods and variables. The methods of an object are the corresponding functions of a class meaning that any class attribute function object defines the methods for objects in that class.

For instance, because **NewClass.greeting** is a function object and an attribute of **NewClass**, **MyObject.greeting** will be a method object.

Exercise62: Creating an Object

```
class NewClass:
    """This is our first class. What it does
    is display a string text and a value of
    variable name"""
    name = str(input("Enter your name: "))
    def greeting (name):


        print ("Hello", name)


MyObject = NewClass() #Creates a new NewClass object
print (NewClass.greeting)
print (MyObject.greeting)
MyObject.greeting() # Calling function greeting()
```

In Exercise62, the name parameter is within the function definition of the class, but we called the method using the statement **MyObject.greeting()**

without specifying any arguments and it still worked. This is because when an object calls a method defined within it, the object itself passes as the first argument. Therefore, in this case, **MyObject.greeting()** translates to **NewClass.greeting(MyObject)**.

Generally speaking, when you call a method with a list of x arguments, it is the same as calling the corresponding function using an argument list created when the method's object is inserted before the first argument.

As a result, the first function argument in a class needs to be the object itself. In Python, this is typically called self but it can be assigned any other name. It is important to understand class objects, instance objects, function objects, and method objects and what sets them apart.

Constructors

In python, the **__init__()** function is special because it is called when a new object of its class is instantiated. This object is also called a constructor because it is used to initialize all variables.

Exercise63: Constructors

```
MyObject.greeting() # class ComplexNumbers:
    def __init__(self, x = 0, y = 0):
        self.real = x
        self.imagined = y


    def getNumbers(self):
        print ("Complex numbers are:  {0}+{1}j".format(self.real,
    self.imagined))
```

```
Object1 = ComplexNumbers(2, 3) #Creates a new ComplexNumbers
object


Object1.getNumbers() #Calls getNumbers() function


Object2 = ComplexNumbers(10) #Creates another ComplexNumbers
object
Object2.attr = 20 #Creates a new attribute 'attr'


print ((Object2.real, Object2.imagined, Object2.attr))


Object1.attr #Generates an error because c1 object doesn't have attribute
'attr'
```

In the above exercise, we have defined a new class that represents complex numbers. We have defined two functions, the **__init__()** function that initializes the variables and the **getNumbers()** function to properly display the numbers.

Note that the attributes of the objects in the exercise are created on the fly. For instance, the new attribute **attr** for **Object2** was created but one for **Object1** was not (hence the error).

Deleting Attributes and Objects

You can delete the attributes of an object or even the object itself at any time using the statement **del**.

Exercise64: Deleting Attributes and Objects

```
class ComplexNumbers:
```

```python
    def __init__(self, x = 0, y = 0):
        self.real = x
        self.imagined = y


    def getNumbers(self):
        print ("Complex numbers are: {0}+{1}j".format(self.real,
self.imagined))


Object1 = ComplexNumbers(2, 3) #Creates a new ComplexNumbers
object


Object1.getNumbers() #Calls getNumbers() function


Object2 = ComplexNumbers(10) #Creates another ComplexNumbers
object
Object2.attr = 20 #Creates a new attribute 'attr'


print ((Object2.real, Object2.imagined, Object2.attr))


del ComplexNumbers.getNumbers


Object1.getNumbers()
```

The error you get when you run the script in Exercise64 shows that the attribute **getNumbers()** has been deleted. Note, however, that since a new instance is created in memory when a new instance of the object is created, the object may continue to exist in memory even after it is deleted until the garbage collector automatically destroys unreferenced objects.

Conclusion

If you have followed the order of this book from the start and have completed the 64 exercises within it, congratulations! You can now refer to yourself as a programmer with 64 programs to back up your claim.

This book has been the perfect launch pad for a beginner looking to get the right foundation in object-oriented programming with the intention to advance to intermediate and advanced topics in programming using Python. Considering how far you have come, you are on the right track to becoming an expert in Python programming—whether you are pursuing it to advance your career or to become a proficient hobbyist coder.

What next?

This book covers all the essential areas of Python every beginner needs to master to create basic programs. However, you have not learnt everything important; there are still classes and objects to learn about, you will need to learn and practice how to use date and time functions, and use exception handlers to deal with errors and exceptions in your code. This book did not even touch database access or CGI programming!

The point is, there is still a lot more for you to do before you can become a proficient Python programmer. The internet is an information-rich resource that you can leverage to practice what you have learnt so far, and reinforce the coding skills this book has imparted in you because they are easy to forget without practice.

Developer communities such as Github and StackOverflow are just two of the many places you can begin to explore and interact with, and learn from, other Python learners and developers. Remember, any time you face difficulty or need assistance of any kind, we will always be ready to help.

Lightning Source UK Ltd.
Milton Keynes UK
UKOW01f0834270617

304143UK00007B/814/P

9 781545 479117